# THE BRIGHT AND SHINING REVIVAL

## An Account of the Hebrides Revival 1948-52

## Kathie Walters

**Good News Fellowship Ministries**
**220 Sleepy Creek Road**
**Macon, GA 31210**
Phone: **(478) 757-8071** Fax: **(478) 757-0136**
**goodnews@reynoldscable.net**
www.goodnews.netministries.org

The Bright and Shining Revival
ISBN 978-1-888081-57-2
Printed in the United States of America
2nd printing

Scriptures were taken from the
King James Version of the Bible. Copyright
1979,1980,1982
BY Thomas Nelson Inc. Used by permission

Published by
**Good News Fellowship Ministries**
**220 Sleepy Creek Road**
**Macon, GA 31210**
**Phone: (478) 757-8071     Fax: (478) 757-0136**
**goodnews@reynoldscable.net**
**www.goodnews.netministries.org**

Kathie's contact information:
kathiewalters@mindspring.com
**www.goodnews.netministries.org/kathie.htm**

# Contents

# Foreword

This book brings me back memories of half a century ago. As a young man keenly interested in revival and recently baptized in the Holy Spirit, I was anxious to know how Pentecost and revival were related. With this in mind I had a distinct urge to go to the Hebrides. I found myself there just as the revival was deemed to be over.

I had the privilege of chauffeuring Duncan Campbell for about a week of what I think was his last campaign on the island of Lewis, and learned much of what had taken place from his own lips. God called me, however, to take the message of Pentecost to the islands subsequent to the revival. The call came as clear as in an audible voice, and I saw the glory of God.

Kathie's book gives a very true portrayal of the feeling of revival as distinct from an intellectual, theoretical description of it. Something of the power and atmosphere of it is converyed in these pages.

I meet again characters I knew so well, most of whom are now with Christ - Coinneach Beag, that man of prayer; John Smith (the Gobha), who was powerfully used not only in the '49 but very particularly in the '39. Barbara's long suffering is over. And Mary MacLean, one of the closest friends I ever had, is with her Lord. Donald McPhail still lives and bravely serves God on a very dangerous foreign field. I was privileged to know some of the great ones of God.

Enough of nostalgia. It is good to look backwards, if looking back spurs us forward - in this case to know more deeply the God they knew and learn something of the secret of their overcoming.

Kathie makes this very plain in her book. She wants the reader to realize something of what God can do in revival, and her tales whet the appetite, but she is interested in spurring this generation to action with a clear understanding of underlying principles. A vital part of her message is contained in one paragraph under the heading 'The Challenge'

> *The wonderful visitation of God to the Hebrides islands, is not only one of the most stirring and faith building events of our generation, but also represents one of the greatest spiritual challenges to us now. Its scenes of divine power reveal the tremendous potential of a genuine move of God in our churches and communities. The pattern of events which led up to the visitation, amplified by the declarations of the Word of God, makes it very evident that what has taken place in the Hebrides can be experienced anywhere else in the world. There is no town, city or village that is exempt from the covenant power of the covenant-keeping God. Was the Hebrides a great city? No! Was the group praying a large company of experienced prophetic intercessors? No! Did they pray for years and years? No! They prayed for five months.*

I close with remembered comments of Duncan Campbell: "Revival is neither more nor less than the impact of the personality of Jesus Christ upon a church or a community. The whole area becomes God-conscious." May revival reign again wherever this book is read.

Rev. Hugh B. Black
Senior Minister of the Struthers Group of Churches
27 Denholm Street
Greenock, PA168RH
Scotland, UK

*Hugh Black graduated from Glasgow University with an Honours degree in History in 1950 and served as Head Teacher of two Greenock secondary schools from 1964 to 1985. He has been a minister of Struthers Memorial Church since its foundation in 1954 and is one of the leaders of the Struthers Movement.*

*He has had wide experience in preaching and lecturing in and beyond his own church circles and has been widely used in evangelism. For over forty years he has pioneered pentecostal teaching in many parts of Britain - seeing literally thousands receive the Baptism in the Spirit. He has also been used in the healing ministry.*

# The Bright and Shining Revival
## An account of the Hebrides Revival
### 1948-1952

## Notes from the Welsh Revival 1904

"This is revival! When men in the streets are afraid to open their mouths and utter godless words lest the judgment of God should fall; when sinners, overawed by the presence of God, tremble in the street and cry for mercy; when, without special meetings and sensational advertising the Holy Ghost sweeps across cities and towns in supernatural power and holds men in the grip of terrifying conviction; when every shop becomes a pulpit; every heart an altar; every home a sanctuary and people walk softly before God - this is revival" (Quote from Rev. Owen Murphy).

Rev. Murphy continues, "The Welsh Revival of 1904 was like a mighty tornado. The Spirit of God swept across the land until mountains and valleys, cities and villages were filled with the mighty manifestations of God. Churches were crowded and meetings went on day and night. Prayer, singing and testimonies would sweep over congregations in torrents, and hundreds turned to Christ. Never in the history of Wales had such indescribable scenes been witnessed."

"Dr. Campbell Morgan, after witnessing the scenes of revival in Wales, returned to Westminster Chapel in London and declared, 'Here is revival that comes from heaven; there is no preaching, no order, no hymn-books, no choirs, no organs, no collections and finally no advertising! Now think of that for a moment! There were organs - but they were silent. There were ministers - but there was no preaching - they were among the people praising God! Yet the Welsh revival is a revival of preaching, for everybody is preaching. No order and yet it moves from day to day, county to county with matchless precision, with the order of an attacking force. No song-books, but- ah me, I nearly wept over the singing! When the Welsh sing they abandon themselves to the singing. No choir did I say? It was all choir.'"

"Wales is ablaze for God, already 50,000 converts have been recorded and the great awakening shows no signs of waning. It is sweeping over hundreds of villages and cities, emptying saloons, theaters and dance halls, and filling the churches night after night with praying multitudes. Go where you will; into the bank; the store; the trains. Everywhere men are talking about God."

Fire Breaking Out

"If you could stand above Wales, looking down over it, you would see the fire breaking out here and there and yonder, and somewhere else, without any pre-arrangement. It is a divine visitation from God - Oh! Let me say this reverently. God is saying to us, 'See what I can do without the things you are depending on, see what I can do through a praying people who are prepared to depend wholly and absolutely upon Me.'"

"Like a tree shaken by a mighty storm, Wales was moved by the power of God until almost every home in the nation felt its impact. Newspapers in bold headlines carried the news of the amazing scenes taking place. So great was the fear of God, and conviction gripped the people, that in some communities crime disappeared. Magistrates were presented with a blank paper; no cases to be tried. And, to commemorate the occasion, they were presented with white gloves! In more than one place the Post office's supply of money orders were exhausted as people sought to make restitution by paying their debts. Saloons and theaters were closed and stores were sold out of Bibles and New Testaments. Members of Parliament, busy attending revival services, postponed their political meetings. Theatrical companies coming into districts found no audience, for all the world was praying."

God Can do it Again

"This is revival - A mighty God moving on behalf of men and women who have cried out to Him. Can God do this again? I believe He is waiting to release His awesome power. He is now preparing the way through dedicated and praying, believing people. There is a time to pray and then there is a time to receive God's answer, for prayer is not a one-way communication. The men and women who prayed in the wonderful revival in the Hebrides Islands got hold of God's promise - and the fact that He was a covenant- keeping God who kept His word. This story is meant to encourage you to do the same as they did - for God has not changed, His word has not been voided - He is still waiting to respond to a praying, believing people who will not let Him go." (*When God Stepped down - from Heaven* - Rev. Owen Murphy).

# The Hebrides Revival 1948-1952

The Hebrides Islands are a small group of islands off the West coast of Scotland. In 1948 -1952, God poured out His Spirit in response to a handful of praying men and women. It doesn't take multitudes to move the hand of God - but those who are determined to 'push through the crowd' and touch the hem of His garment.

The First Stirring

At a meeting of the Church of Scotland, in Stornaway, a group of men discussed the awful condition of the church in their communities. The worldly places were crowded and the churches were virtually empty. The young people had just about disappeared, and it seemed that many churches were about to close their doors. No one at the meeting dreamed that this would be the preliminary meeting of an amazing spiritual awakening.

Among the many people who were concerned about the state of the church, was a small group of 7 men from Barvas, the district that was to become the center of the revival.

4

## The Barn

The men agreed to meet in a small barn by the side of the road to pray. They were given the revelation that God was a covenant- keeping God who had made covenant promises! "If this is true," they reasoned, "We can enter into this covenant, and if we keep our part then He must keep His. Has God given us a covenant promise for revival?" Immediately the words of 11 Chronicles 7:14, came to them, *"If My people which are called by My Name, shall humble themselves and pray, and seek my face and turn from their wicked ways, then will I hear from heaven and forgive their sin and <u>heal their land</u>."*

That same night they entered into a solemn covenant with God to pray for the community and to humble themselves in prayer until revival came. For months they prayed and waited on God. Three nights a week they wrestled and prayed until 4am or 5am. Finally, one night, a young deacon arose from his knees and began to read Psalm 24, *"Who shall ascend into the hill of the Lord? Or who shall stand in His Holy place? He that has clean hands and a pure heart - he shall receive the blessings of the Lord."*

In response to this searching challenge from God they fell upon their knees in confession and re-dedication and began to pray even more earnestly. An hour later three of them were laying prostrate on the floor - they were exhausted. By five o-clock revival had come! The barn was suddenly filled with the glory of God, and the power that was let loose filled that little barn, and shook the whole community.

Duncan Campbell with Christine and Peggy Smith, Barvas. Peggy was blind. They believed that revival was coming.

*(Permission of Faith Mission Magazine / Edinburgh)*

The Praying Sisters

Around the same time, in a little cottage in the village of Barvas, two elderly sisters - Peggy and Christine Smith - were also praying. Peggy was almost blind, and Christine was bent over with arthritis. They were 84 and 82 years old. They also had been seeking God for revival, and to them came the promise, "I

6

will pour water upon him that is thirsty, and floods upon the dry ground."

One night, knowing that the others had gathered together to pray in the barn, the sisters gathered around their little peat fire to spend the night in prayer. Suddenly Peggy had a vision of the church, crowded with young people. She sent for the minister, Rev. James Murray MacKay, and told him what God had shown her, asking him to encourage his elders and deacons to come together for special times of waiting upon God.

God's Choice

On the same night when the presence of God visited the barn, the glory swept into the little cottage and God spoke to the two women, revealing to them the name of the man God wanted to use in the visitation - The Rev. Duncan Campbell, a Presbyterian minister and a great man of prayer.

A wire was sent to Duncan Campbell, who was ministering in the Highland town of Skye, but it was discovered that he was already booked for another meeting. He sent a reply, "It is impossible for me to come at this time, but keep praying and I will come next year." When the reply was told to the sisters they answered, "That is what man has said, but God has said that He will be here in two weeks." In the meantime Duncan Campbell's meetings in Skye were canceled, due to the fact that the tourist board had monopolized the accommodation for a convention. Within two weeks he was in Barvas!

## Duncan Campbell comes to Barvas

Duncan Campbell crossed the Minch in the *Loch Seaforth*. He was planning to stay for 10 days in Barvas. Little did he know what awaited him! As the ship docked and Duncan stepped ashore, he was met by the Rev. James MacKay and two of his elders. One of the elders greeted him and asked, "Mr Campbell, are you walking with God?" "Well, at any rate, I can say that I fear God," was Duncan's reply.

## The First Meeting

The first meeting was held in the old parish church. Duncan Campbell preached from Matthew 25 on 'The Wise Virgins'. Many people had gathered in great expectancy, but nothing exceptional happened at that meeting. Some of the congregation moved to a nearby cottage to pray. Duncan Campbell appeared discouraged and so one of the deacons went to him and said, "Don't be discouraged, it is coming. I hear the rumbling of heaven's chariot wheels."

At the cottage about thirty knelt in prayer and began to travail before the Lord. About 3 am God swept in and a dozen or so were laid out prostrate on the floor, speechless. Something had happened - God had moved into action as He had promised. Revival had come and men and women were about to find deliverance.

As the group left the cottage they found men and women seeking God. Lights were burning in the homes along the road - no one seemed to be thinking about sleep. Three men were found laying by the roadside in a torrent of conviction, crying out for God to have mercy on them! The Spirit of God was moving into action and soon the parish of Barvas was to be stirred from end to end.

The Second Night

The second night Duncan preached this time on the 'The Foolish Virgins'. Buses came from the four corners of the island, people crowded into the church. Seven men were being driven to the meeting in a butcher's truck when suddenly the Spirit of God fell on them in great conviction and all were saved before they reached the church building! As the preacher preached his message, tremendous conviction swept down. Tears rolled down the faces of the people and men and women cried out for mercy from every corner of the church. So deep was their distress that some of their cries could be heard outside in the road. A young man beneath the pulpit cried out, "Oh hell is too good for me."

The meeting closed when the people began to move out. As the last person was leaving a young man began to pray under a tremendous burden of intercession. He prayed for three quarters of an hour and as he continued to pray people kept gathering outside until there were twice as many outside as there had been inside. When the young man stopped praying the Elder gave out Psalm 132 and, as the great congregation sang the old hymn, the people streamed back into the church again and the meeting continued until 4am.

The moment the people took their seats, the Spirit, in great conviction began to sweep through the church, and hardened sinners began to weep and confess their sins.

The Police Station

As the meeting was closing someone excitedly hurried to the preacher, "Come with me! There's a crowd of people outside the police station; they are weeping and in great distress. We don't know what's wrong with them but they are calling for someone to come and pray with them."

The minister described the scene outside the police station. "I saw a sight I never thought possible. Something I shall never forget. Under a starlit sky, men and women were kneeling everywhere, by the roadside, outside the cottages, even behind the peat stacks, crying for God to have mercy on them."

Nearly 600 people, making their way to the church, suddenly experienced the power of God falling upon them in great conviction, and like Paul on the road to Damascus, fell to their knees in repentance.

Revival had come in power - for five weeks it swept across that one parish. Duncan Campbell conducted four services every night; in one church at 7pm, in another at 10pm and a third at midnight; back to the first one at 3am - then home between 5-6am - tired, but happy to be in the midst of such a wonderful move of God.

True Intercession

Peggy and her sister shared in the revival. When the minister visited them next day they told him how they had been wrestling in intercession for the revival. They told how they had been battling - holding on to the promise. "We struggled through the hours of the night refusing to take 'no' for an answer. Had He not promised? Would He not fulfil it? Our God is a Covenant-keeping God and He must be true to His Covenant engagements. Did He fail us? Never! Before the morning light broke we saw the enemy retreating and our wonderful Lamb take the field." The minister asked them what supported their strong faith and Peggy replied, "We had a consciousness of God which created great confidence in our souls which refused to accept defeat".

Although they were confined to their little home, nevertheless they prayed through the villages, cottage by cottage. They were so close to the Spirit that they knew where the hungry and seeking souls were to be found.

After this, the revival began to spread to other towns, and what had happened in Barvas began to happen in other places.

Men and women throughout the island began to plead to God in desperate intercession and prayer for revival. The Spirit's power began to increase.

God Visits Arnol

Arnol was a small community which came within the path of the spiritual tornado. Because of the spiritual indifference it was reckoned that hardly a young person darkened the doors of any house of God; the Sundays being given to drinking and poaching, etc. News of the revival spread and an opposition meeting was held. Although the church was crowded, it was because many people came from various parts of the island - there were very few actually from Arnol.

The little band of prayer warriors made their way to the farmhouse to plead the promises of God. Just after midnight Duncan Campbell asked John, the local blacksmith, to pray. John rose to his feet with his cap in hand and prayed a prayer that will never be forgotten by those who were present.

In the middle of his prayer he stopped and raised his right hand to heaven and continued, "Oh God, you made a promise to pour water on the dry ground, and Lord it's not happening." He paused again and then continued, "Lord, I don't know how the others here stand in your Presence; I don't know how these ministers stand, but Lord, if I know anything about my own heart, I stand before you as an empty vessel, thirsting for thee and for a manifestation of Thy power." He halted again and after a moment of tense silence cried, "Oh God your honor is at stake; and I now challenge you to fulfill your covenant engagement and do what you promised to do."

The Prayer of Faith

Here is a man praying the prayer of faith that heaven must answer. There are those in Arnol today who will verify the fact that while the brother prayed, the dishes on the dresser rattled as God turned loose His mighty power. Then wave after wave of divine power swept throughout the room. Simultaneously, the Spirit of God swept through the village . People could not sleep and houses were lit all night. People walked the streets in great conviction; others knelt by their bedsides crying for pardon. As the men left the prayer meeting the preacher walked into a house for a glass of milk and found the lady of the house with seven others down upon their knees, crying out for God.

Within 48 hours the drinking house, usually crowded with drinking men of the village, was closed. 14 young men who had been drinking there were gloriously converted. Those same men afterwards could be found three times a week with others down upon their knees before God, praying for their old associates and for the spread of revival. It was in this village that, within 48 hours, many young people had surrendered their lives to Christ, and could also be found in the prayer meetings!

Among those converted the following night was a young boy of 16, named Donald Mcphail. Donald became an outstanding prayer warrior and was asked often to pray in the meetings. One day Duncan Campbell found him in the barn with his Bible open. When interrupted he quietly said, "Excuse me a little Mr. Campbell, I'm having an audience with the King."

The Power of Prayer - Bernera

Some of the most vivid outpouring came when Donald was asked to pray. In the police station one night in Barvas, he simply stood up, clasped his hands together and uttered one word - "Father." Everyone melted into tears as the presence of God filled the station. In Callenish, he prayed until the power of God laid hold of those who were dead in sins, transforming them into the living stones in the temple of God.

One of the  most outstanding anointings of prayer happened when Donald Mcphail was in Bernera, a small island off the coast of Lewis. Duncan Campbell was assisting at a Communion service; the atmosphere was heavy and the preaching difficult, so he sent to Barvas for some men to come and help in prayer.

They prayed, but the spiritual bondage persisted, so much so that half-way through the sermon, Duncan stopped preaching. Just then he noticed Donald, visibly moved under a deep burden for souls. He thought, "This boy is in touch with God, and living nearer to the Savior than I am." He said, "Donald, will you lead us in prayer?" The young lad rose to his feet and made reference to the fourth chapter of Revelation which he had been reading that morning. "Oh God, I seem to be gazing through an open door. I see the Lamb in the midst of the Throne, with the keys of death and hell at His girdle." He began to sob, then lifting his eyes toward heaven, cried, "Oh God there is power, let it loose!" The Spirit of God swept into the building and the heavens were opened. The church resembled a battlefield. On one side many were prostrated over the seats weeping and sighing; on the other side some were affected by throwing their arms up in the air in a rigid posture for an hour. God had come!

*When he was 16, Donald McPhail was often called upon by Duncan Campbell to pray during the Hebrides meetings.*

## Outside the Church

Outside, startling things were taking place. The Spirit of God was sweeping over the homes and the area surrounding the village, and many people came under the convicting power of the Spirit. Fisherman out in their boats; men behind their looms; men at the pit bank; a merchant out in his truck; school teachers examining their papers were gripped by the power of God and by 10 o'clock the roads were streaming with people from every direction, making their way to the church.

As the preacher came out of the church the Holy Spirit swept in among the people in the road like a wind. They gripped each other in fear. In agony of soul they trembled; many wept and some fell to the ground under great conviction of sin. Several men were found laying by the side of the road in such distress that they could not even speak - yet they had not been anywhere near the church!

So great was the supernatural moving of God that most of the homes did not escape the conviction of the Spirit, and the routine of business was stopped, that the islanders might seek the face of God like Ninevah of Bible days. The town was changed, lives and homes transformed, and even the fishing fleet, as it sailed out into the bay, took with it a Precenter, to lead them in prayer and worship singing.

You Can't Get Away from God

*Duncan Campbell*, in his biography by Andrew Woolsey, describes the revival as "A community saturated with God." He goes on, "The presence of God was a universal, inescapable fact: at home, in the church and by the roadside. Many who visited Lewis during this time became vividly conscious of the spiritual atmosphere before they reached the island."

The scripture, *"Whither shall I go from your Spirit, or whither shall I flee from your Presence?"* took on a very real meaning. One night a man went to the manse in great concern for his soul. He was brought ito the minister, who asked him, "What happened to you, I have not seen you in any of the services?" "No," he replied, "but I can't get away from the Spirit."

Another man was frightened by what his sister reported of the revival. He actually prayed that God would keep Duncan Campbell away from his village; he did not want to be converted. But Duncan arrived in his village. The man kept well away from the meetings at first, but eventually gave in. In the service Duncan Campbell made a reference to 'those who had made vows to God while they were in danger at sea.' "That's me ( His boat had been torpedoed during the war), my sister must have told him about me. I'll settle with her when I get out of the meeting."

But conviction seized him and increased as the day went on. Duncan Campbell visited him and prayed with him. That night the burden was unbearable and when Duncan asked the seekers to come to the vestry for prayer, he rushed to the room to give his life to God. He had difficulty understanding the message of salvation, but eventually broke through. He saw at his feet the chains and locks of sin which had bound him. It was so real that he leaped up in ecstasy, thinking he was leaping straight to heaven. Later, he was met by one of the elders by the roadside and a circle of light seemed to envelope them. Looking up, he found himself looking into the face of the Savior. Not everyone had that same spectacular experience, but it was not uncommon.

Led of the Spirit

People were sensitive to the Spirit and were willing to be led by God. A woman out in the field, milking a cow, was suddenly led to go to the house of a neighbor to tell of Christ. Another young man, driving a bus, was burdened to stop and plead with the passengers to repent. He was sure that someone was hearing God's call for the last time and they would not be on the return journey. The warning went unheeded and a young man died in tragic circumstances.

Duncan Campbell was very sensitive to the Spirit; often he would know when people were going to be saved, and which house they lived in.

Another prayer warrior who lived miles away from Tarbert told the time and day when the revival reached that village. He said, "I was in the barn when suddenly the place was filled with light, I knew that God had broken through in Tarbert."

A schoolmaster, also a man of prayer continued for weeks with only a couple of hours sleep, snatched after classes each day. Groups of Christians, unwilling to return home, would gather at the sea-shore or roadside, singing praises and sharing together what God had done.

Coinneach Beag

Duncan Campbell told this story of Coinneach Beag. Coinneach was man of prayer, a deeply spiritual man. He had indicated to Duncan that the revival would break out in Carloway at a particular time, and was with him in the first meetings. There was a particularly hard meeting, and Duncan Campbell stopped preaching, sat down and called on Coinneach to pray. He stood up and began to intercede. He prayed for about half an hour. Suddenly, Coinneach, who had been speaking to God, said, "Will you excuse me for one moment Lord, while I speak to the devil."

Mr Campbell opened his eyes to see Coinneach with his fists raised, as a fighting man, and he addressed the devil with some purpose. He demanded that he go from that place. Suddenly, it was as if a bomb exploded. God flooded in. Revival had come! God reigned and Coinneach sat down. The Spirit did His own glorious work that night. Mr Campbell said that the next time he saw Coinneach, he was fast asleep on the bench. His work was done. And he slept the sleep of the just.

Encouragement

Hugh Black ministered in the Hebrides Islands toward the end of the revival. He tells of a small meeting in a house where there was discouragement, owing to a lot of opposition. Three of the group left the house and Hugh sat with his head in his hands. Suddenly there was the sound of running feet, about midnight, when the streets were normally deserted. The three who had gone, were back at the door. Hugh says that he has never seen people in such a condition as they were in. They were breathless, unable to speak, as if they were in shock. One of them said, "There is a man out there."

Hugh thought they must have been pursued in the street and he moved to go out and see. The lady in the group stopped him. "It's not that," she said, "He is in white - it is Christ." They finally told the story. They had gone down the street and one of them had noticed a band of light in a very clear sky. It formed the shape of a cross, and one of the others gripped her arm and said, "Look at that." As they watched, out from the cross there came a luminous cloud and from it the figure of Christ appeared, with a hand stretched forward. The three went down on the pavement. Another said, "We couldn't look again because of the glory." Then I ( Hugh Black), said, "I am going out to see."

"We all went outside. For a couple of  hours I saw supernatural lights, balls of light moving low in the sky. I felt the effects of that experience in my body for  2-3 weeks." (*Revival-Personal Encounters by Hugh Black*)

Ness

One night in Ness, the crowd was so great that the people spilled out of the house into a field and sang and sang. An old woman who was bitterly opposed to the revival came out and shouted angrily at the first man she met. "I wish you would all go home and let me get some sleep." Towering over her, the man put his hands on her shoulders and replied, "Go away home yourself, *Cailleach,* you've been asleep long enough." She took off as fast as her rheumatics would allow!

Duncan's preaching was bold and plain - he spoke of sin and the penalty of it. It was prophetic preaching, not diplomatic preaching and hearers were always confronted with a choice.

The deep conviction of sin characterizing the movement was enhanced by Duncan's insistence on declaring the true knowledge of sin and judgment. At times his voice was drowned with the sound of people weeping uncontrollably. He would often have to stop preaching because of the distress manifested by those who were being convicted.

A man who had resisted the ministers for a long time was cycling down the road when he suddenly saw balls of fire being spit up on the road in front of him. In the fields, at their looms, men in boats were suddenly prostrated on the ground.

Duncan knew the danger of allowing human sympathy to interfere with the convicting work of the Spirit. He offered no superficial comfort to those in distress.

When it seemed hard to break through, as in Rev. Angus MacFarlane's church, Duncan would send for the praying men from Barvas. The presence of these praying men in the meetings, was of great comfort and encouragement to Duncan. He once said, "More was wrought through the prayers of these men than all the ministers put together, including myself."

Supernatural Manifestations of God

So overwhelming sometimes was the Presence of God, that people were afraid to open their mouths lest they utter words that would bring judgment upon themselves. People walked quietly before God and, as in every true revival, many a shop became a pulpit, many a home, a sanctuary, and many a heart became an altar.

A visiting minister of Lewis declared, "So tremendous has been this sense of an awareness of God, that I have known men out in the fields, others at their looms, so overcome that they fell prostrate on the ground! One outstanding trophy of grace was converted while crossing a field. He testified, 'So great was the sense of God's presence, that even the grass beneath my feet and the rocks around me seemed to cry out, `Flee to Christ for refuge.'"

Even the most hardened sinners and notorious characters of the district have literally been found laying helpless by the roadside, stricken with conviction as in the great Welsh revival of 1904. Another remarkable feature was the persistent nature of the Spirit in following men and women until decisions were made.

Trying to Escape from God

It was known that some people even left the Island altogether, in order to avoid the searching presence of God. Such was the case of a young man who found that, like Jonah of old, it was impossible to escape from God. One night, after being spoken to about his personal need of salvation, he was griped by conviction and he began to tremble. "This won't get hold of me," he muttered. "I'll get away from here and drink my way out of it." Entering the drinking place he ordered a drink, but to his consternation he overheard a group of men discussing their own great need and fear of being lost. He trembled even more. "This is no place for a man who wants to shake this off," he growled. "I'll go over to the dance and I'll dance my way out of it." He hadn't been in the dance hall for very long when a young lady came up to him exclaiming, "Oh! Where would eternity find us if God should strike us dead tonight?" Tremendous conviction swept down upon the young man and he surrendered himself to Christ.

## Angels

Donald Smith told me that in 1949 the angels were heard singing at Barvas and at Point, and throughout the Island. One of the elders who heard them was Colin Nicolson. At Kinloch, Angie Maclead, one of the elders from the church, also reported hearing the angels singing as they were going over to Barvas. One night after a prayer meeting in Shader the angels were heard singing, so the people followed them until they stopped. They went into a house nearby and some women were on their knees praying to the Lord to have mercy on them. These dear ladies became shining lights in the village until they died.

Hugh Black has had several experiences of angelic assistance when he was ministering in the Hebrides. Five young ladies reported seeing lights going down chimneys and on one of the churches in Shader. Donald Smith told me that recently he had heard the sound of angels singing as he drove past the place where the barn was, where the men used to pray. His car was full of the sound of angelic song.

## The Sisters Request

The sisters, Peggy and Christine, continued to pray for the revival. One day Peggy sent for Duncan Campbell, asking him to go and hold meetings in a small isolated village. The people of this village were not in favor of the revival. Duncan questioned the wisdom of her request. "Besides," he added, "I have no leading to go to that place." She turned in the direction of the voice, her sightless eyes seeming to penetrate his soul. "Mr. Campbell, if you were living as near to God as you ought to be, He would reveal His secrets to you also." Duncan felt like a subordinate being reprimanded for defying his General. He humbly accepted the rebuke as from the Lord and asked if he and Rev. MacKay could spend some time praying with them. The sisters agreed. As they prayed together, Peggy prayed, "Lord, you remember that you told me this morning, that in this village You are going to save seven men who will become pillars of the church of my fathers. Lord, I have given your message to Mr Campbell, but it seems he is not prepared to receive it. Oh Lord, give him wisdom because he badly needs it!" "All right Peggy, I'll go the village," Duncan said. Peggy replied, "You had better - and God will give you a congregation."

The Seven Men

Arriving in the village about 7 pm, they found a large single-storey house, already crowded to capacity with many others outside. Duncan gave out a Bible text, "The times of this ignorance God winked at, but now commands all men everywhere to repent." When he was through preaching, a minister beckoned him to the other end of the house to speak to a crowd of people who were weeping and mourning over their sins, among them - Peggy's seven men!

Letter from Donald John Smith concerning the two sisters (9th September 2000)

*Dear Kathie,*

*the Smith sisters in Barvas always humbled themselves under the mighty hand of God, earnestly seeking His face in prayer, then bowing before Him in worship and praise. It was a blessing to me and a joy to be praying with these dear sisters at the throne of grace.*

*They were concerned with the souls of men and where they would spend eternity.*

*It grieved them when Christian people filled most of their conversation with every day secular events instead of being centered around the Lord.*

*Certainly, those of us who experienced God's mighty river still carry the hallmarks of that great spiritual awakening.*

*Their home on earth was a humble home, but they were seeking one to come whose builder and maker is God. They were just living from day to day depending on the Lord for their daily food. They were seeking first the Kingdom of God and His righteousness -believing that all other things would be added unto them.*

*Their main talk was on revival and they believed that the Lord was to pour down His spirit in a mighty way and they saw this fulfilled before they went home to Glory.*

*"Those who turn many to righteousness shall shine as stars forever and ever."*

*We believe that they are now in the presence of the Lord where there will be no more pain and no more parting. They awoke in His likeness and they are satisfied.*

*What a difference it makes in our lives to be a Christian; the love, the joy; the fellowship of the Lord's people in His house; and the comfort of God's word, going out in power, anointed by the Holy Spirit as a word in season to the soul that is weary. He accepts us as we are - nothing in our hand we bring, but just simply to the cross we cling. His blood is covering us and when the Lord sees the blood, He passes over us.*

*My prayer is for the lost to come to Christ, while He is still on the throne of mercy. We want the lost over there with us - the ones we loved here on earth.*

*In Christ we have everything - the riches of eternity. May we all have the place of many mansions as our eternal home.*

*Sincerely, Donald John (Smith) Upper Shader, Isle of Lewis*

In some districts there was hardly a soul who was not affected by the revival. One man who had very little time for God was driving along the road when he suddenly saw before him a vision of hell. Startled and afraid, he jammed on his brakes, pulled his car to the roadside, then, kneeling down he surrendered his life to Christ.

*Left - Donald Smith, the author of the letter, was converted during the Hebrides revival. God told him to "go and tell My mighty works." Right - Donald John Smith - Ballantrushel. Donald is the son of the blacksmith who God used many times to pray down the power of God.*

## Conviction

Sometimes conviction rested upon sinners for days, causing great distress of mind. Such was the case of a man so convinced of his godless life, and seemingly unable to get peace of mind in spite of repentance, that he rushed down to the sea-shore, and hiding behind the rocks, prepared to commit suicide. A young woman in her home, while kneeling in prayer, had a vision of this man: God showed her exactly where the man was and what he was about to do. Rising quickly, she called her minister, instructing him where to find the unfortunate man. The minister arrived just in time to save the man, not only from physical death, but also eternal hell.

Some of the men who were saved became great trophies of God's grace. One of them was out in the field working, when great conviction fell on him. He began to tremble violently. "You're not a sissy, what's the matter with you?" he said to himself. The voice of God seemed to thunder into his soul. "You are a poacher and a Sabbath-breaker." He knew what God meant - he had been breaking the law - poaching. He was a drunkard, a real godless fellow, and this was a new experience to him. Feeling miserable and wretched because of the burden of sin, he went along to the church and was gloriously converted.

Another man, sitting in a hotel, was met by God in the same amazing way. Stretching forth his hand to pick up a beer, he suddenly became conscious of God's presence. He began to tremble and great conviction took hold of him as the voice of God began to thunder in his soul, and he put down his beer. Shortly afterwards he was gloriously converted to Christ and became a great witness for Jesus.

Visions

During the revival a young woman was used in powerful visions and trances. One night she had a vision of a woman in agony of soul twenty miles away. Duncan was informed that he ought to go and see this woman. Immediately he motor-cycled to the village, found her, brought her deliverance, and introduced her to the Savior. Not one message given by this young visionary proved false. Duncan did not encourage or discourage these trances, but he recognized it was God and warned people not to interfere or associate it with any demonic activity.

The revival of 1939

There are accounts of the revival which broke out in the Hebrides in 1939. It appears to have started somewhere around Point. Not as much is known of this revival, as of the later one (1949). The war came and there was a scattering of the people. But the accounts that are available seem to speak of this revival as a more powerful revival in some ways. Hugh Black was told that the Spirit of God would suddenly sweep into a room and half the people would be in a trance-like state - swept up into the realm of the Spirit. The people in that revival certainly were in faith to pray and believe for the move of the Spirit in 1948-52.

Hugh Black in his book, *Revival - Personal Encounters*, tells of a woman named Barbara. Barbara was a great prayer warrior who birthed, through intercession, many souls into the kingdom. One man, Colin, told Hugh Black of his experience when Barbara prayed for him. He was in a pub, in Stornaway, one night, not interested in the revival. He was raising the glass to his lips when he suddenly had a vision of Barbara standing before him. The man put down his glass and hastily made his way back to Shader. On the way he knew that he had to pass Barbara's house. Sure enough, as he passed, who should step out into the street, but Barbara!

Hugh asked Barbara questions about the revival. "Oh yes," she replied, "Revival is wonderful - for some people. But for us - there were a number of us, women, who weren't in the meetings." Mr Black was startled to learn these people were not in the meetings. They did not have time to be in the marvelous meetings. "The breath of the Spirit," she said, "Would come and it was like women in childbirth. We would fill up and up with the breath of God, and we would be in an agony, and suddenly a soul would be born into the kingdom, and there would be relief as the new soul was born. Then the weight would come again, and we would fill up again and again and others would be born. And so it went on again and again." These women carried the burden of prayer and through God birthed people through to salvation.

Mary MacLean

The praying women in this revival, like Barbara, were powerfully used by the Holy Spirit. Mary, whose own testimony is written below, was also wonderfully used to prophesy and pray. Mary would be caught away in the spirit often and God would reveal His secrets to her.

Mary MacLean comes from a people who are given to visions, and visions are not strange to these people. She lives in a land where the veil is thin and she has led a godly life. This account concerns a vision Mary had just prior to the second world war, and which is related to it :

On 10th March, 1939, Mary had a baby daughter, and she felt herself strongly surrounded by the presence of God. Two nights later the first vision came: Mary related this to Hugh Black:

*"There came a rushing wind. I was away (in the spirit). I don't know how long I was away - but the graves opened. I thought it was the last day - Judgment Day. I don't know how long I was away, but when I came back, I said, 'Oh Lord, if it's Judgment Day, everyone here is unconverted,' and the power came for praying for all those unconverted people all over the world. The whole world came upon me. And I was shaking, and I prayed that I would go away again in the Spirit."*

*"I was just waiting. And there came a rushing wind again. I was taken up. It was the sea that came in front of me then. And I went down to the bottom of the ocean, and the ships were laying there, and the bodies of men were there. Oh. What a place! When I came back I was shaking and baby was beside me."*

*"When the war broke out in August, that was when I got a revelation about what I was seeing, when I was down at the bottom of the sea, and saw the bodies there."*

*The War*

*"I thought, 'This is the war now, that I have seen - the ships down there in pieces, and the bodies!' I was afraid that I would go away again . And I wondered what I would see next.  What would be revealed to me?"*

*"I decided not to tell anyone of anything I had seen. They would think that the Lord was going to take me away, and they would be so upset."*

"Now the Communions were coming (at the local church), 15th March, and baby was born on the 10th. I would preach to the unconverted that a revival was on its way. I told them to be out day and night at the meetings and not to miss anything; a great revival was coming. And, Oh they were thinking something was wrong with me - they didn't know what was coming upon me; 'Oh! Be out, (at the meetings) be out morning and night!' I said."

"Pressure was coming upon me and prayer was coming upon me. I thought the Lord was going to take me home and I wasn't worried for the family. I knew the Lord would get someone to look after them. I was all prepared to be taken away. Oh, the presence of the Lord was so strong, I thought no one could stay in this cold world without the presence of the Lord."

Revival is Coming!

"And there was a girl who lived near me, and she helped me with the baby. 'Oh! Hetty!' I used to say, 'be out morning and evening. Revival is going to come!' And after the Communion, she came and said, 'I was out to every meeting and no revival came!' 'The revival is coming,' I said, 'You keep out (at the meetings) revival is coming.' Anyway, the Communions in Point came about the end of March. And I was waiting for the revival, when the power would come."

Mary spoke some things about her family and then continued:

"I had started going into visions again. Some of them were long visions, and I needed my mother's help to look after the baby. The longest vision I've been in was one in which I went cold, as if I were dead. And Oh! The vision I saw there, a vision of heaven and hell. The people were plunging into hell as if they were sheep plunging over a precipice, and I was hearing the gnashing of teeth and the crying. I saw the flames going through the people and I thought, 'With the furnace that was coming out of hell, that there wasn't a hair of my head that wasn't singed with the furnace.'"

"But then a vision of Christ - I couldn't take my eyes off Him, I couldn't blink. The vision of heaven was so wonderful, and the brightest day here is like darkness compared with the light that's there in heaven."

"While I was away so far (in the spirit), my sister told my mother, 'Mary has passed away, and she won't come back now. She's cold and I have taken clothes to put on her, and a white sheet, to go over her until the coffin comes.' My sister was so upset. I was cold, as cold as a dead person. I don't remember how long my mother said I was away (in the Spirit). But a crowd was in the house thinking that I had passed away, and there was a wake going to be on."

"There was one sister in Lower Shader (village), a very dear soul, that was under the power like myself. She was my cousin. Her brother was an elder in the Free Church, and he went home and told her, 'You won't see Mary again, Mary has passed away.' She didn't believe it!"

*She has passed away!*

"My sister told my mother, 'You must believe Mary has passed away this time.' 'No I don't believe it. I have often seen Mary going away like this (in the spirit).' 'Oh, but Mum, she's stone cold all over and I can't find a pulse anywhere.' After that, after a long while, I felt streams going through my body, through my arms and through every part of me, like thin streams warming me up. Then I said to my sister, 'Oh Annie, will you make me a hot water bottle?' Annie said that was the most wonderful thing she had ever heard! I couldn't move at this stage - I couldn't move my arms or legs, but bit by bit I was warming up ... and I came back to this life."

"My Mother asked me, when she saw I was fully back, 'Oh Mary, did you see anything about our own house?' 'I didn't see anything, but I know this - you will be left alone. You will be left alone in this house.' She couldn't understand how that could happen. Where were the boys going - the three of them?"

*The Bottom of the Sea*

"The war hadn't broken out then. Later my three brothers were taken away to the war. They went in August. I was with my mother all the time. It was when the war broke out that I finally realized what I had seen in the vision at the bottom of the sea, with the ships and bodies - it was all connected to the war.

"I was finally able to come home with the children; my husband and brothers were away to the war. One

34

night when I was on my knees praying for my brothers, and everyone in the whole world, I saw the ship that the youngest one was on; it was a trawler. It was in half - it was split in half - and I saw him in the water. With what I saw, I got up from my knees and started thinking. 'It must been that I was praying for him, and got afraid that this would happen!'"

"I started walking the floor. 'Oh, what was this?' Word that he was missing came, and I told people that this happened two weeks ago (the night was clear in my memory). The postman left letters here for me to break it to my mother and father that he was missing. But then word came that he was not found among the survivors, and I told them, 'Well, this happened two weeks ago.' They said, 'How do you know that?' 'I've seen it,' I said, 'I've seen it with my eyes, I know this.'"

"Next my other brother died on board ship with, I think, a gastrated stomach. There was a month between them, that was all - and he was buried at sea. Seemingly, he had been converted. He had talked to a man from Carloway, who was with him on the boat, seemingly a Christian. My brother had said, 'When we get home after the war, you'll go down to our house, so that it will be easier for me to go out to the weekly meetings ( a sign of conversion in the revival) with you.'"

Communion

"Soon after that, an urge came on me to go to back to my own church, at a Communion time, and I said,

'Oh Lord, I can't go there. How can I go there? I have not been going to that church, and how can I venture out at the Communions?' But the pressure of the Lord came, and I had to go. But I wouldn't do this without going first to the elders, and saying that I was coming to take communion."

(The elders finally allowed her to go to the Communion table)

She continued..

"And I did go to the Communion table. But the power came after that and I couldn't venture out to this church. At every opportunity I went back to the Church of Scotland. What a battle - you can understand what I was going through. But the power was so strong from the Lord.

"The presence of the Lord was so wonderful and I was saying, 'Oh well as long I am under this pressure from the Lord, He will give me all the words I need. I don't need to worry.' I stayed at the next Communion, but I was so much under the power of God, that they had to bring the bread and wine to me. I wasn't afraid to speak to the elders openly in front of the minister. The minister asked, 'Why didn't you come to church after you had communion?' 'Because when the power of God came on me I was going out of the body, and I didn't want to upset any of you. When the power of the Spirit came I was in visions'. They made no comment on this. 'Oh well, you can come any time you feel the Lord is leading you to come to the table.' So that was my experience with them!"

Mary's church (Free church of Scotland) did not appear to accept the manifestations of the Spirit - hence her reluctance to attend the services there. Instead she went to the meetings of the Church of Scotland.)

Hugh Black questioned Mary (*The Clash of Tongues and Glimpses of Revival*) further about the visions she received about the war. She identified the house in which she was when the news of the fall of France was broadcast on the radio. The news profoundly depressed the people who were gathered there. She threw her hands up in the air and glorified God, indicating that France had to fall before the victory could come. She had foreseen the defeat of Germany and the ultimate triumph of the Allies. At first, the company of people, thought they had a traitor in their midst, as she was glorifying God because France had fallen. But she went on to explain future events, (that France had to fall first before the ultimate fall of Germany). The presence and power of God became evident, and the whole company was affected. It was a very wonderful night.

Counter-attack

There were many converts during the '39 revival, before the counter-attack came. Mary had been hopeful that the whole community might be converted. The attack did not come from outside, but from within her own church. Had the leaders moved with God, she felt, the outcome would have been even more glorious.

*The Hebrides Revival first erupted in this Church of Scotland building in Barvas.*

Note: (from Hugh Black's book, *The Clash of Tongues with Glimpses of Revival:*

"I have found in Lewis a great quickening of spiritual faculties. In a peculiar way the veil between this world and the spiritual world seems to be very thin. God and the things of God become very real. The sense of evil at times too can seem very intense........."

The Praying Men (1948-52)

Whenever Duncan Campbell was in the islands after that, he never left without visiting the praying men who had helped so much in the revival, and with whom he had such an affinity of spirit. He marveled at their discernment and worldwide vision. They prayed for nations they knew little about - but they heard from God and obeyed the calling of the Spirit.

The Effects of Visitation

The impact the revival made in the districts that were visited brought much lasting fruit, but as in other revivals, there were districts that were not touched.

Quoting from the Keswick Journal in 1952 - "More people are attending prayer-meetings in Lewis today than attended public worship on the Sabbath day before the outbreak of revival. Social evils were swept away as by a flood in the communities touched by this gracious movement. Men and women are living for God. Family worship is in nearly every home; five or six prayer meetings a week in the parish; pastors and elders building up men and women in the faith. Of all the hundreds who turned to Christ in the first wave of the Holy Spirit, until now, only four young women have ceased to attend the prayer meetings." The converts were numbered by their attendance at the prayer meetings. Absence from the prayer-meeting meant a doubted conversion! (Here is a standard very few churches would dare to adopt. If we judged our converts or church members by their attendance at prayer meetings, what would happen?)

During the revival over 80 new hymns were written and, although the emphasis of the Holy Spirit was on the conviction of sin and warnings of judgement, almost every hymn was centered on the love of God.

The happy people of the Hebrides Isles had made the discovery of a lifetime. They discovered the reality of God and the great things he had been waiting to do for them.

The Secret of the Visitation

The Hebrides revival was a manifestation of God! Something greater than organization, something more wonderful than simply a new approach to evangelism, this was God at work - God in action, independent of special personalities. But behind the irresistible power of God, there was a "secret." One minister and seven members of his church, in a little wooden barn by the side of the road, who were prepared to stand in faith, praying and believing, and who got hold of God - that revival might come.

What was the secret of these men? - Faith in a Covenant-Keeping God

These men were fully persuaded that revival lay within their grasp through the covenant promises of God. Had not God Himself declared, *"If my people, who are called by My name shall humble themselves and pray, and seek My face, and turn from their wicked ways; then I will hear from heaven and forgive their sin, and heal their land"* (11 Chron. 7:14).

A covenant is an agreement, binding on both parties. The praying men knew that if they kept their part of the agreement, then the agreement was binding upon God - for He is not a liar. His word must come to pass and they could absolutely depend upon it. God has promised revival; therefore He is waiting to send it. If this was true, then revival did not depend on God, but on His people keeping the conditions of the covenant! Staking everything upon this fact, three times a week the men met in the little barn by the roadside to keep the conditions of the covenant promise and hear from heaven.

Each night, as they knelt in the straw, they would renew their faith by remembering the promise, and declare before the Presence of God the certainty of the coming revival. Nothing, including the long weary months of waiting, could weaken their confidence that God would keep His promise.

"If My People..."

"If My people which are called by My Name, will humble themselves..." God is Holy and humanity must humble itself before Deity. Before man can stand on Holy ground, he must be clean. This drama unfolded itself as one of the men in the barn slowly rose from the straw and began to read from Psalm 24.

"Who shall ascend into the hill of the Lord? Who shall stand in His holy place? He that has clean hands and a pure heart; who shall not lift up his soul unto vanity, nor sworn deceitfully; he shall receive the blessing of the Lord."

Like flames falling from the lips of a Holy God, every word seemed to burn into the hearts of the men gathered to do business with Him. Before the challenge of this declaration, unhesitatingly, they fell to their knees in unreserved dedication and surrender to God. They were prepared to meet every demand, whatever the personal cost might be, that revival might come. The price - brokenness before God, an emptying of self, a forsaking of sin and habits.

Prevailing Prayer

Every revival that has broken upon the face of the earth has been preceded by men and women upon their knees travailing before God. Undeterred by cold and the discomforts of the barn; undeterred when there appeared to be no answer; undeterred by the fact that no one else seemed concerned about revival and the world was as godless as ever, they travailed and prayed. Kneeling in the straw or upon their faces in agony of soul, they cried before the throne. No half-hearted, sentimental, religious, half- doubting prayers to which the church is so accustomed today, and which accomplish so little. These men wrestled with God, drawing into the spiritual conflict every power and energy they possessed.

The men who had covenanted to stand for revival PRAYED! They stormed the throne of God. God imparted to them a burning passion of the lost. Confidence in God gripped every word that fell from their lips. What depths of reaching out to God! They prayed until they travailed and travailed until they prevailed. They prayed until God answered. Travail must always precede "prevail." *"When Zion travailed she BROUGHT FORTH"* (Is 66:8).

The Challenge

The wonderful visitation of God to the Hebrides Islands is not only one of the most stirring and faith building events of our generation, but also represents one of the greatest spiritual challenges to us now. Its scenes of divine power reveal the tremendous potential of a genuine move of God in our churches and communities. The pattern of events which led up to the visitation, amplified by the declarations of the Word of God, makes it very evident that what has taken place in the Hebrides can be experienced anywhere else in the world. There is no town, city or village that is exempt from the covenant power of the covenant-keeping God. Was the Hebrides a great city? No! Was the group praying a large company of experienced prophetic intercessors? No! Did they pray for years and years? No! They prayed for five months.

Gathered with the men in the barn was their elder/ minister, a symbol of every minister who is prepared to join with his people in seeking the face of God. Standing in the shadows behind the revival was another minister, Rev. Duncan Campbell, the man God chose to preach during this time of divine visitation.

Burdened because of the spiritual indifference of the ungodly; grieved at the decline of spiritual life in the churches; feeling utterly helpless in the face of such a challenge, he knelt in his study crying to God.

Suddenly, but quietly, the Spirit of the Lord came upon him, and before him there appeared a vision of a dying world plunging into an abyss of eternal darkness, and multitudes of men and women speeding on to Christ-less graves. Then came the revelation that was to transform his ministry - God was a covenant-keeping God who made covenant promises to His people! Like a great flash of light, he suddenly saw that there was a great realm of potential, power and blessing within his grasp through the covenant promises of God. He could enter into a covenant with God. If he kept his part, he could have more of the power of the spirit in his ministry. From that moment, through surrender to the Lord and constant waiting on God, he entered into a ministry that was to cause men and women to feel the impact of the Presence of God. Fearlessly preaching the judgments of God against sin, and emphasizing the faithfulness of God, he saw hundreds, stricken by great conviction of sin, turned to God.

The Power of God Vs Formalism

Formalistic preaching never raised the dead. Only a demonstration of Divine power can do that. Such it was in the days of Whitfield, when it was a common sight for sinners to cry out. Under his anointed preaching, some were struck pale as death and fell prostrate to the ground; others sank into the arms of friends.

Born in New Hampshire in 1810, John Wesley Redfield, an old-time evangelist had great and powerful demonstrations of the power of God in his ministry. One time after weeping before God, he heard God speak to him, "You may prepare for the greatest display of My power that you have ever witnessed in this church."

That night, before he had finished preaching, people flocked to the altars crying for mercy. Another time, the church was suddenly filled with an awful sense of the presence of God. Like a thunderclap the power of God broke upon the meeting and hundreds, panic stricken with fear, crowded the altars pleading for mercy

The biggest hindrance to revival is not Communism or any other "ism", but dead religion that gives people a substitute for the Presence of God. Churches and leaders pray for a visitation of God, but draw back in fear when God begins to show up in power. People look for the presence of God, but when He comes, dynamic and sensational things happen, and many leaders do not like the sensational! But, how can you have the demonstrations of God's Spirit  without sensational things happening? Jesus' ministry was certainly sensational. How can you raise the dead, cast our devils, bring miracles of healing and turn the world upside down, and not disturb the world around you? To quote Rev. Owen Murphy, "When Jesus healed the sick, and raised the dead; when Peter and John brought deliverance and healing to the lame man outside the temple; when the Spirit of God was poured out upon Jerusalem on the day of Pentecost, causing thousands to be converted - did not these acts cause sensation? Certainly they did. Yet these acts were not fanaticism. They were the acts of a miracle-working God manifesting His divine power, that the eyes of the people might be turned to Himself".

The Bible is full of accounts of sensational acts of God. I think the parting of the Red Sea must have been a pretty sensational sight, don't you? Or Jesus walking on the water would be mind-boggling. As Owen Murphy points out, "God cannot work where there is unbelief, but He requires our faith as a vehicle to work through. The Old Testament cries out, 'Ye have limited the Holy one of Israel,' and its echo in the New Testament is, 'Because of unbelief, He (Jesus) could do no mighty works.'"

Faith

Shall we be guilty of unbelief through our fear of God working in an unorthodox way? We are happy to read in the Bible about Moses, Joshua, Elijah and the Apostles, but what would have happened if they had doubted God? Nothing! If fear of the sensational had gripped them, we would never have read about the parting of the Red Sea, the walls of Jericho falling down, or fire falling upon Carmel. If Jesus and the Apostles had not dared to step out and obey God, we would never have read about the prison doors opening, the blind seeing, the deaf hearing, and the lame walking!

If we desire to see the same kind of revival today as they saw in Wales in 1904, in the Hebrides in 1948, and in many other times in history, we must rid ourselves of our unbelief and complacency. We must get hold of God and, in obedience, do what He says. We must believe He is a covenant-keeping God. He is not a liar. He promised to come and "heal our land" if we would keep our end of the promise - to humble ourselves and pray, and to seek His face and turn from our wicked ways. GOD'S RESPONSE IS, "THEN WILL I HEAR FROM HEAVEN AND FORGIVE THEIR SIN AND HEAL THEIR LAND."

These must be men and women who are not casual seekers of God, but those who mean business, like the men in the barn, who will not let go until they receive the confirmation that He has heard according to His own covenant.

Letter and testimoney from Donald John Smith, Lower shader, Isle of Lewis - August 2000

*Dear Kathie,*

*I had the privilege of praying with Christine and Peggy Smith Barvas the two praying ladies mentioned in Rev Duncan Campbell's book. I also used to read the Bible with them every time I called at their home. The fragrance of heaven was in that home.*

*There was a lot of men and women in the community praying as well. When Zion travails, children are born unto the Lord. Blessed are the ones whose desire is to frequent the gates of Zion, for the Lord's desire is to translate sinners from the Kingdom of darkness unto the Kingdom of light, so that in His light they also may see light.*

People would be praying behind airns of stone, behind peat stacks in Barvas, and they were not frightened of who would hear them. One night Mr Campbell was passing a barn in Barvas and he heard the people praying. He stopped for a while and listened, but they were not praying for him or the revival in Barvas, but for Greece. Mr Campbell asked them why they were praying for Greece and they couldn't explain why.

Mr Macauley, a retired minister, still living in Bernera, Lewis, told us afterwards a ship was being built in Belfast and it was for Greece. When it was ready, one of the mates on that ship (from Lewis) went over to Greece. They heard that a revival was also taking place in Greece at that time - so who can explain the working of the Lord. His ways are not our ways, neither are His thoughts our thoughts.

Donald Smith continues......A SHORT TESTIMONY

I had the privilege of being brought up in a Christian home where the Bible was read in the morning and at bed-times. Grace for every day what we had to face to that day was our daily prayer to the Lord. In the day school we started with Psalm 23 every morning. "The Lord is my shepherd, I shall not want." My parents were Christians; the whole family were Christians. The love of Christ and the warmth of the gospel was felt in the home and it reached out into the community. It was wonderful giving your life to the Savior in the midst of a revival when we felt the dew coming down from heaven. We were brought up in the nurture and admonition of the Lord. Love answering love as love comes from above.

When we went out into the world among the heathen we did not learn their ways. The gospel is the greatest message that mankind has ever heard, or ever will hear, for Christians hold in their hands and hearts the true happiness of millions around the world. We have hope beyond the grave. We have forgiveness and a purpose in life.

When we look back, we see the path that we had been treading and we notice that it's been a downward grade. It could have been pride, earthly success or even prayerless nights. When we repent of our sins we have a change of mind and a change of direction. Our heart must be broken at the cross of Calvary. He longs for hearts that will love Him, and the amazing thing is that He will supply this love to those who are humble enough to receive it. "You has He quickened who were dead in trespasses and sins" (Eph.2:1)

I was thankful to the Lord for seeing generation after generation giving their hearts to God. "One generation shall praise thy works to another, and show thy mighty acts."

"I will honor thy glorious majesty" (Psalm 145:4-5).

We pray that the family bonds that unite us here on earth will not be broken on the other side. We cannot leave the lost and alone, we want them over there with us. All the branches of the vine will be gathered together into the family of God. Our heart goes out to those who are still outside the fold. We love them and Christ loves them. We see so often the mortal remains of our dear brothers and sisters being laid to rest in the grave. The very dust of the earth from which we are formed will one day be gathered together to be a glorious resurrection body presented without blemish and without spot at the great white throne. Washed in the blood of the Lamb.

"What a day it will be when my savior I see, in that beautiful city of gold.

When the trumpet of the Lord shall sound and time shall be no more,

And the morning breaks eternal bright and fair.

When the saved of earth shall gather over on the other shore,

And the roll is called up yonder - I'll be there".

My prayer is that we'll all be there.

God's richest blessing,

Donald John Smith

24 Upper Shader, Isle of Lewis, HS2 ORQ Scotland UK

# Sources

*When God Stepped Down from Heaven*  Rev. Owen Murphy

*Duncan Campbell*  Andrew Woolsey. Hodder and Stoughton
The Faith Mission, Edinburgh, Scotland

*Revival: Personal Encounters*  Hugh Black. New Dawn Books, Greenock, Scotland

*The Clash of Tongues with Glimpses of Revival* - Hugh Black
New Dawn Books, Greenock,  Scotland


Personal Testimony as told to Kathie Walters from:

Donald Smith, Ballantrushal, Isle of Lewis

Donald John Smith, Upper Shader, Isle of Lewis

Donald Mcphail, Isle of Lewis, Scotland.

Hugh Black, Greenock, Scotland

*Hugh Black's books available through*

*Good News Ministries, Macon GA 31210*

# Kathie Walters books:

***Living in the supernatural*** - Kathie believes that the realm of the Spirit, the supernatural life, heavenly visitations, angels etc are meant to be a normal part of the life of every Christian.

***The Spirit of False Judgement*** - How to make judgements according to the mind and heart of the Lord - not according to how you see and hear in the natural realm.

***The Visitation*** - Two accounts of visitations Kathie had. She was lifted into heaven and shown the relationship between Jesus and His betrothed.

***Parenting - By the Spirit*** - Learn how to train your children by listening to the Holy Spirit and not your emotions.

***Celtic Flames*** - Accounts of the wonderful and powerful ministries of the early Celtic Fathers of the Faith like Patrick, Brendan, Cuthbert, Brigid etc.

***Columba - the Celtic Dove*** - Accounts of the ministry of Columba of Iona. His prophetic gift, miracle ministry and angelic visitations

***Angels - Watching Over You*** - Did you know that the angels of God are sent to minister to you and with you. They are meant to be a normal part of the life of every Christian

***Elitism & the False Shepherding Spirit*** This book discusses Control, Manipulation, False Shepherding Spirit, Spirit of Abortion, Grief and how to be set free from them.

***Seer's List*** - Explanation of the Seer anointing and how it "works."

*Health Related Mindsets* - Various mindsets the Lord has shown me that can bring sickness.

*Progest... What?* – Information on progesterone cream.

For Celtic CD's - call 800-300-9630 for catalogue.

Kathie ministers in churches, conferences, and seminars.

She believes the realm of the Spirit, the supernatural realm, the angels, miracles etc. are meant to be a normal part of the life of every Christian.

The religious spirit prevents God's people from receiving all the inheritance God has for them.

For further information on Kathie's ministry, write or call:

Good News Ministries

220 Sleepy Creek Rd.

Macon GA 31210

800 300 9630

www.goodnews.netminstries.org/kathie.htm

E-mail: kathiewalters@mindspring.com

# Books by David Walters

**Kids in Combat: for Parents and Teachers** - How to train children and teens to be radical for God, a must for youth and children's pastors.

**Equipping the Younger Saints** - Teaching children and youth the Baptism of the Holy Spirit and spiritual gifts (Parents, teachers, children/youth pastors).

**Children Aflame** - Amazing accounts of children from the journals of the great Methodist preacher John Wesley in the 1700's and David's own accounts with children and youth.

**The Anointing and You** (How to Understand Revival) What we must do to receive, sustain, impart, and channel the outpouring for renewal - revival, and to pass it on to the younger generation.

**Worship fur Dummies** - David Walters calls himself a dummy in the area of praise and worship, but he knows the ways of the Holy Spirit.

**Radical Living in a Godless Society** - Our Godless Society really targets our children and youth. How do we cope with this situation?

Children's Bible Study Books
**Armor of God** - Children's illustrated Bible study on Ephesians 6:14-18 (ages 6-14 years).

**Fruit of the Spirit** - Children's illustrated Bible study on Galatians 5:22 (ages 6-14 years).

**Fact or Fantasy** - Children's illustrated Bible study on Christian apologetics. How to defend your faith (ages 8-15 years).

**Being a Christian** - Children's illustrated Bible study on what it really means to be a Christian (ages 7-14 years).

**Children's Prayer Manual**- Children's illustrated study on prayer (ages 8-14 years).

**The Gifts of the Spirit**- Illustrated Bible study on the Gifts of the Spirit (ages 7 years - Adult).

# Divine encounters for Children and Youth

The Seminar "Raising a Generation of Anointed Children and Youth" is available on Video or DVD. It has over five hours of teaching for Pastors, teachers, Parents, children and youth. The set includes four videos or 2 DVDs, a syllabus and David's well-known "Kids in Combat" book.

We also offer "Kids in Combat" and a teaching syllabus for $8.00. This allows you to make available the book and syllabus for each family.

For information on David Walters' Seminars:

"Raising a Generation of Anointed Children and Youth."

Or, "Equipping the Younger Saints" conferences

Please call or write:

Good News Fellowship Ministries

220 Sleepy Creek Road

Macon, GA 31210

Phone: (478) 757-8071 Fax: (478) 757-0136

goodnews@reynoldscable.net

www.goodnews.netministries.org

For information on Kathie's exciting Ireland and Scotland Tours- including visiting the 5th Century Christian Celtic Sites, contact:
Good News Fellowship Ministries
220 Sleepy Creek Road
Macon, GA 31210
Phone: (478) 757-8071 Fax: (478) 757-0136
goodnews@reynoldscable.net
www.goodnews.netministries.org/kathie.htm